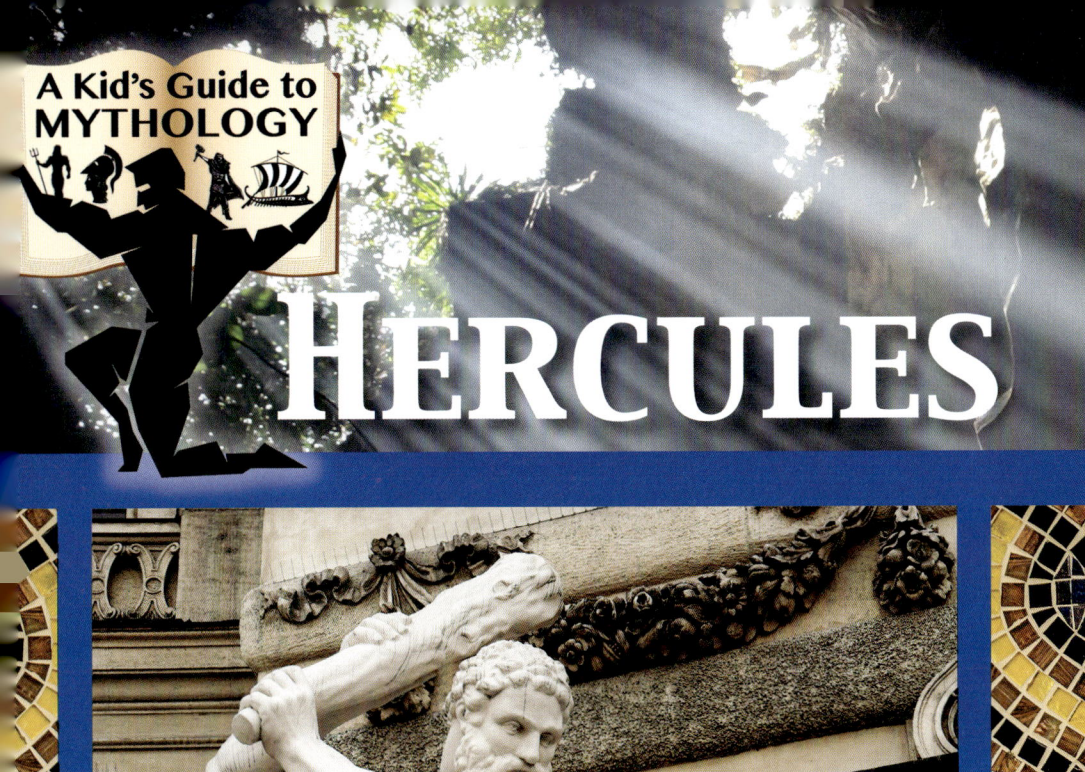

A Kid's Guide to
MYTHOLOGY

HERCULES

JOHN BANKSTON

Mitchell Lane
PUBLISHERS
P.O. Box 196
Hockessin, DE 19707
www.mitchelllane.com

Mitchell Lane
PUBLISHERS

Copyright © 2016 by Mitchell Lane Publishers, Inc. All rights reserved. No part of this book may be reproduced without written permission from the publisher. Printed and bound in the United States of America.

Printing   1   2   3   4   5   6   7   8

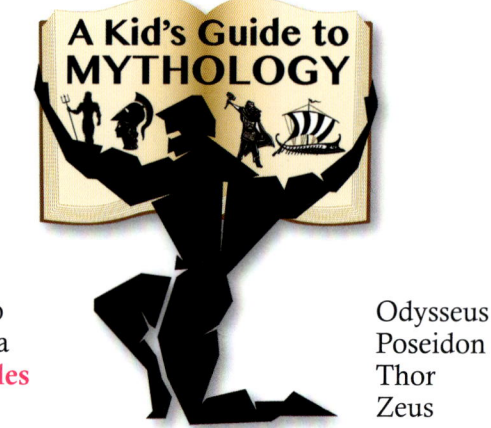

A Kid's Guide to MYTHOLOGY

Apollo
Athena
Hercules
Jason

Odysseus
Poseidon
Thor
Zeus

Library of Congress Cataloging-in-Publication Data
Bankston, John, 1974– author.
  Hercules / by John Bankston.
      pages cm. — (A kid's guide to mythology)
  Summary: "Myths were stories that explained the mysteries of the ancient world. Few myths have endured like the myth of Hercules. Half man and half god, Hercules was the strongest person who ever lived. He fought scary, powerful creatures—and won. Yet he was never strong enough to over-come his own anger. The story of Hercules is the story of love lost and battles won."— Provided by publisher.
  Audience: Ages 8-11.
  Audience: Grades 3-6.
  Includes bibliographical references and index.
  ISBN 978-1-61228-996-0 (library bound)
 1. Hercules (Roman mythological character)—Juvenile literature. 2. Heracles (Greek mythological character)—Juvenile literature. 3. Mythology, Greek—Juvenile literature. 4. Mythology, Roman—Juvenile literature. 5. Gods, Greek—Juvenile literature. I. Title.
  BL820.H5B27 2016
  398.20938'02—dc23
                                                                                   2015005444
eBook ISBN: 978-1-61228-997-7

PUBLISHER'S NOTE: The Internet sites referenced herein were active as of the publication date. Due to the fleeting nature of some web sites, we cannot guarantee they will all be active when you are reading this book.

To reflect current usage, we have chosen to use the secular era designations BCE ("before the common era") and CE ("of the common era") instead of the traditional designations BC ("before Christ") and AD (anno Domini, "in the year of the Lord").

DISCLAIMER: Many versions of each myth exist today. The author is covering only one version of each story. Other versions may differ in details.

PBP

Contents

Chapter 1
Epic Battle 5
Rome 9

Chapter 2
A Hero Is Born 11
History or Just a Story? 19

Chapter 3
Labors of a Hero 21
The Olympics 27

Chapter 4
Final Labors 29
Constellations 35

Chapter 5
Death of a Hero 37
Hercules in the 21st Century 43

Chapter Notes 44
Works Consulted 44
Further Reading 45
On the Internet 45
Glossary 46
Index 46

Words in **bold** throughout can be found in the Glossary.

This sixteenth-century statue of Hercules (top) by Florentine artist Baccio Bandinelli shows the hero's victory over the fire-breathing Cacus.

1

EPIC BATTLE

Cacus (KAY-kuhs) breathed fire and ate people. He was a dangerous thief, twice the size of anyone else. No one had survived a fight with Cacus. One night, he stole some of Hercules's (HUR-kyuh-leez) cows.

Hercules was the strongest man on earth. On the night that Cacus stole his cows, Hercules had stopped for some rest during a journey from Spain. He was traveling with the cows so he could bring them to a king. Just to get the cows, he had fought their owner Geryon (GEH-ree-uhn)—a giant with three bodies that were attached at the waist. He had also fought Geryon's two-headed guard dog. Now it looked like he would have to fight Cacus.

At first, Hercules was confused. The cows were gone but he did not know where they were. Their hoof prints went in all directions. Then he heard a "moo." He followed the sound and realized the cows were hidden inside a cave.

Cacus had pulled a giant rock in front of the cave's entrance so that Hercules could not get in. So Hercules went to the top of the cave and removed the roof. Shocked, Cacus began to breathe fire and smoke so that it was impossible to see. This only angered Hercules more. A Roman writer named Virgil (VUR-juhl) put the

CHAPTER 1

story in writing during the first century BCE. He explained, "Hercules lost all restraint, in his fury at this: he hurled himself down through the fire with a headlong leap, to the point where the smoke rolled thickest and billowed about the huge cave in eddying black clouds. He laid hands on the **ogre** . . . got a quick hold, knotted him double, and throttled him . . ."[1]

Hercules had won. The cows were safe.

No man had ever beaten Cacus. But Hercules was more than a man. He was half god. He was also a mythological character.

Hercules and Myth

Over two thousand years ago, a Greek writer named Plato (PLEY-toh) first used the word "mythologia." He used this word to describe stories that were created and told about people and gods.

Myths are more than just stories though. In ancient times, people believed these stories were true. The stories gave explanations for many of the things that they could not explain.

Today we know why thunder and lightning sometimes strike, and what causes disasters like earthquakes and hurricanes. Even so, these things can be scary. But thousands of years ago, no one understood what caused the ground beneath them to sometimes shake. People did not know why a mountain would suddenly explode. Myths explained these events.

The gods and goddesses in myths were not promised their power for all of time. In Greek and Roman myths, there were violent wars for power. In one of these wars,

EPIC BATTLE

the ruling group of gods called the Titans (TAHYT-nz) fought against a younger group, the Olympians (uh-LIM-pee-uhnz). The Olympians won. They were led by Jupiter (JOO-pi-ter), who was known as Zeus (ZOOS) to the Greeks. His wife (and sister) was named Juno (JOO-noh)—or Hera (HEER-uh) to the Greeks.

For many years, these stories were not written down. As they were told and retold, they changed like gossip whispered in a classroom. Around three thousand years ago, a Greek poet named Homer included some of the stories in two written **epic poems**. Those poems, the *Iliad* (IL-ee-uhd) and the *Odyssey*, included Hercules's adventures.

Myths often happened in real life places. The Olympian gods lived atop Mount Olympus (uh-LIM-puhs), a mountain in Macedonia (mas-ih-DOH-nee-uh). A war was fought in Thessaly (THES-uh-lee). Hercules was born in Thebes (THEEBZ) and served a king in Mycenae (mahy-SEE-nee). All of these places were in the country of Greece.

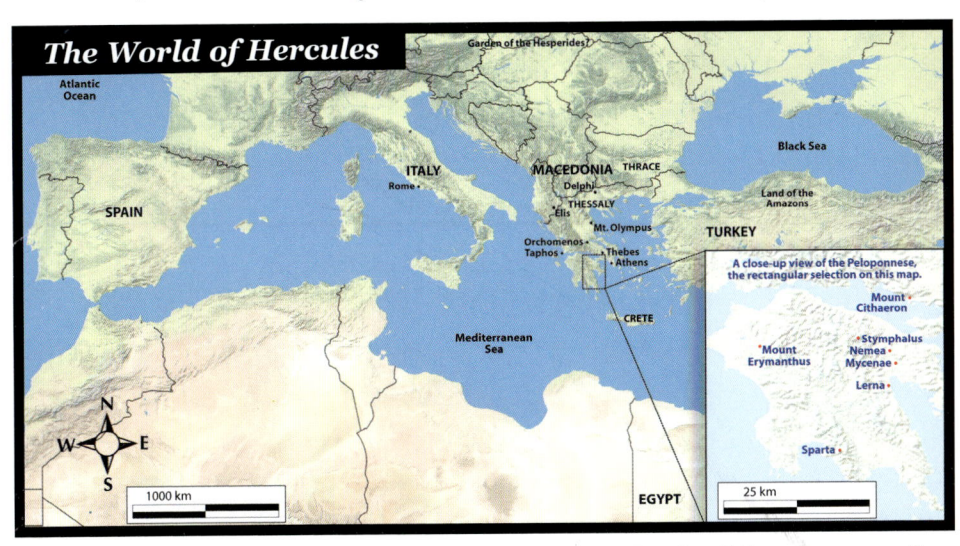

Many of the places visited by the mythological hero Hercules actually existed, as shown by this map.

7

Chapter 1

Myth Meets History

The land of Greece is located in southern Europe, with thousands of miles of coastline along the Mediterranean Sea. Isolated by water and mountains, the people there were usually happy to stay in their small towns, ruled by their local king. Around 750 BCE, things began to change in ancient Greece. Tiny villages grew into powerful **city-states**. City-states were independent; each one had its own rules. Athens became well-known for its art and poetry. Sparta became famous for its well-trained soldiers. City-states sometimes worked together to fight against an enemy. But they also fought each other.

As tales about gods and heroes were being written down, Greeks traveled to Rome and shared their stories. Heracles (HER-uh-kleez) was a character in Greek mythology. In Rome, he was called Hercules.

Hercules was very popular in Rome. In some stories, he fought Cacus near Rome's Palatine Hill. A shrine was later built there honoring Hercules. At the time that Hercules visited, Rome was nothing more than a small village. But that small village became an empire. The Roman Empire eventually controlled not only Greece but the lands where countries like Spain, England, Turkey, and Egypt are today. Most Romans enjoyed stories about a hero who was a great soldier. In Rome he was seen as a protector of soldiers and sailors. The Greeks and Romans had many stories about gods visiting people. Humans were called mortals—those who could die. When a god or goddess had a child with a mortal, the boy or girl was half-human and half-god. This could be very difficult, as Hercules quickly learned.

Rome

The ancient city of Rome had many things in common with the cities that exist today. Although there were not cars or electricity, there were paved roads, tall buildings, and running water. In Rome, concrete was made with water, lime, and volcanic ash. Today concrete buildings are held up with rebar, steel bars that are placed inside concrete to give it more strength. In ancient Rome, rebar was not used. Yet some Roman buildings have survived for more than two thousand years. Most modern structures need regular repair just to last fifty.

Paved roads built by the Romans stretched across Europe. They included sidewalks and mile markers. Some are still used today.

By 312 BCE, Rome's water was delivered by a system of **aqueducts**. These canals were built to connect natural springs outside the city to homes and public buildings in the city. The Aqua Claudia brought water to Rome from a spring forty-three miles (sixty-nine kilometers) away. The canals ran downhill, crossing over hills and across valleys.

Although the rich lived in large homes with clean drinking water, life for the poor was very hard. Many lived in five-story-tall buildings that took up a city block. Because they were surrounded by noisy roads, the buildings were called *insulae* (IN-suh-lee), meaning "islands." Running water did not reach most of these buildings.

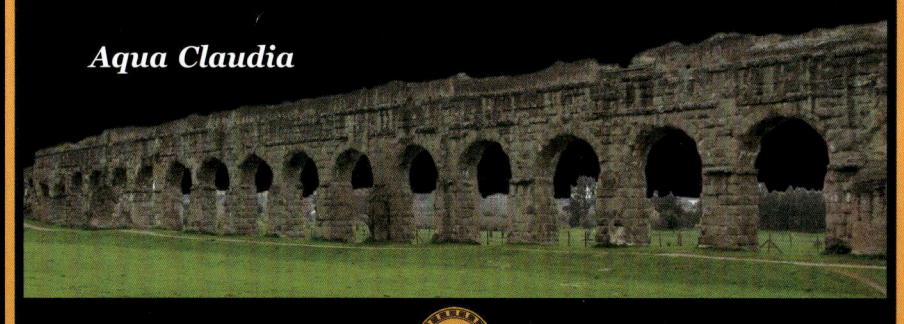

Aqua Claudia

Hercules's mother Alcmene is illustrated on a krater—a large vessel used for holding mixtures of water and wine in Ancient Greece.

2
A Hero Is Born

There was trouble in the kingdom of Mycenae. A group of men from the nearby islands of Taphos had killed King Electryon's (eh-LEK-tree-uhn) sons and stolen some cattle. The king was going to get his cattle back. Before he left, he promised that when he returned, his daughter Alcmene (alk-MEE-nee) could marry his nephew Amphitryon (am-FI-tree-uhn). The couple would be in charge of the kingdom while he was gone. This made Electryon's brother Sthenelus (STHEN-uh-luhs) very angry. He wanted to rule Mycenae himself.

King Electryon soon returned with his cattle, and Amphitryon helped unload the cows from the boat. One cow ran toward Amphitryon, ready to attack. He threw his club to stop it. The club bounced right off the cow's horn and landed on King Electryon's head, killing him instantly.

Alcmene knew that her father's death was an accident. But Sthenelus was not so forgiving. He threw Amphitryon out of the kingdom and took over the throne.

Amphitryon and Alcmene traveled to Thebes, a city-state in Greece. But Alcmene wasn't ready to marry her boyfriend just yet. First, he would have to kill her brothers' murderers. Amphitryon agreed, and he set out to do just that.

Chapter 2

Jupiter watched it all. He thought Alcmene was very pretty and he wished he could be her husband. But Jupiter was already married. So instead of marrying her, he made himself look like Amphitryon.

Jupiter left when the real Amphitryon returned. By then, Alcmene was pregnant. Jupiter would be the boy's father.

The god was very proud. When Alcmene was ready to give birth, Jupiter said that if a child related to Perseus (PUR-see-uhs; Alcmene's grandfather) was born that day, then he would rule Mycenae. Jupiter's wife Juno was very angry. She made sure another of Perseus's grandchildren was born first. Eurystheus (yoo-RIS-thee-uhs) was that child, and he later became king.

Alcmene gave birth to twins. One boy, Iphicles (IF-i-kleez), was Amphitryon's son. The other was Jupiter's child. He would be called Hercules.

Growing up Hercules

From the very beginning, Juno made Hercules's life hard. When he was still a baby, she sent two snakes to kill him. Tiny Hercules grabbed the deadly creatures and squeezed them to death.

Amphitryon knew Hercules was not his son. He still gave him the best of everything. He taught him to drive a chariot. Chariots were carts with two wheels that were usually pulled by four horses. The rider stood up and held the horses' reins. Chariot racing was very popular in both Greece and Rome.

Hercules also learned how to fight with a sword. He learned how to wrestle. A king named Eurytus (YOUR-eh-tuhs) even taught him **archery**. According to some

A Hero Is Born

stories, Hercules later learned hunting, medicine, and law from Chiron (KAHY-ron). Chiron was a centaur: half man, half horse.

Hercules was athletic. He was a better fighter than other boys and he was a faster rider, too. But he wasn't good at everything. In ancient Greece, boys were expected to learn how to sing and play an instrument. Hercules didn't like music class. His teacher Linus (LAHY-nuhs) was the brother of a well-known musician. Hercules was learning to play the lyre, a U-shaped instrument that looks a bit like a small harp.

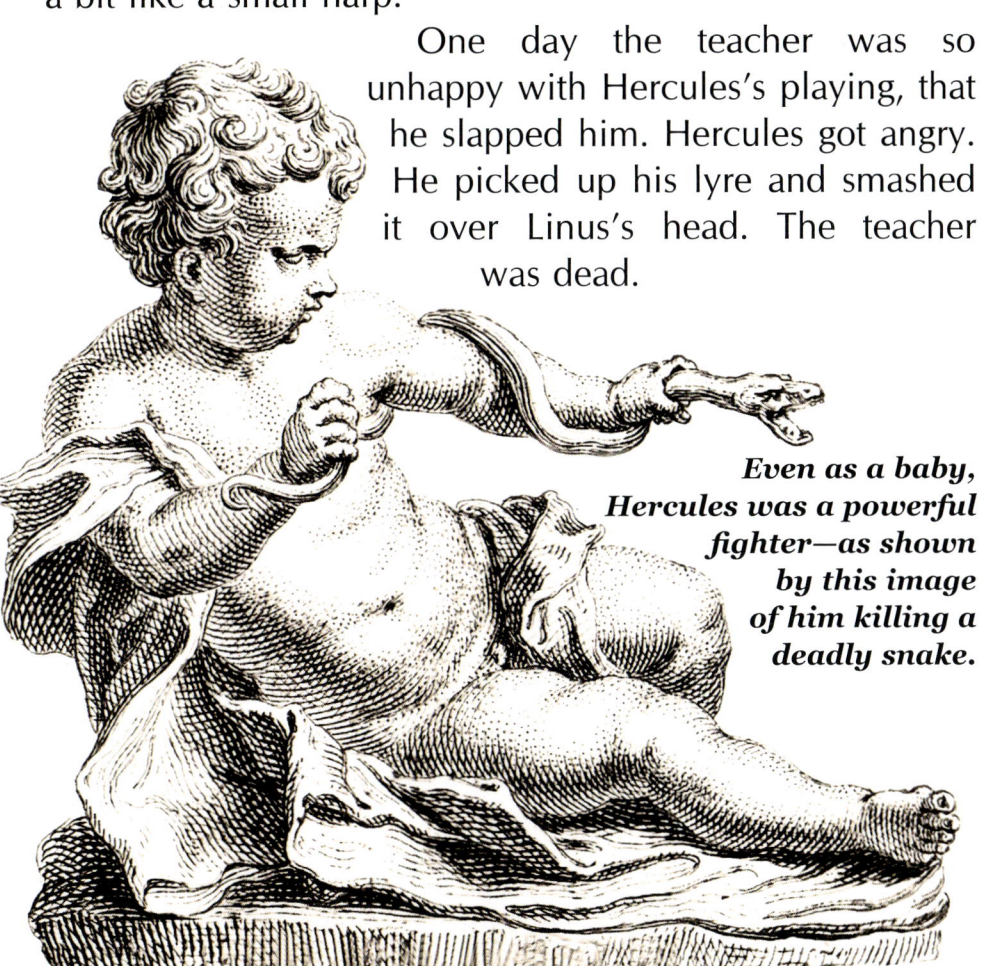

One day the teacher was so unhappy with Hercules's playing, that he slapped him. Hercules got angry. He picked up his lyre and smashed it over Linus's head. The teacher was dead.

Even as a baby, Hercules was a powerful fighter—as shown by this image of him killing a deadly snake.

Chapter 2

Hercules was barely a teenager, and he was charged with murder. He told the court he should not be punished because Linus had hit him first. It was self-defense. The court agreed.

Amphitryon was worried. Hercules had killed a full-grown adult. To keep him out of trouble, Amphitryon sent his stepson away. Hercules moved to a cattle ranch for a life of hard work and early mornings. He loved it.

This krater illustrates Chiron (right), the centaur who taught Hercules hunting, law, and medicine. Chiron is shown alongside a woodland creature called a satyr (left).

The Young Warrior

The Greek historian Apollodorus (ah-pol-oh-DOH-ruhs) wrote that before Hercules was eighteen, "Even by the look of him it was plain that he was a son of [Jupiter] . . . he flashed a gleam of fire from his eyes; and he did not miss, neither with the bow nor with the **javelin**."[1]

He was, in other words, the perfect hunter.

In the woods near Mount Cithaeron (si-THEER-uhn), a lion was eating the livestock. King Thespius (THES-pee-uhs) begged for help from the skilled hunter. Hercules agreed, but on one condition. He didn't want money; instead he wanted to date the king's daughters while he was there. The king had fifty daughters. Hercules dated every one of them!

The lion was sneaky. It was hard to find. After searching for almost two months, Hercules finally found it. He had no trouble killing it.

After taking care of the beast, Hercules was ready to go home. On the way to Thebes, he passed a group of men who had been sent by the Minyans (MIN-yuhns). Thebes had lost a war with the Minyans of Orchomenus, and they demanded that Thebes give them one hundred cattle every year. The group was going to collect.

Hercules thought this was unfair and he let the men know how he felt. He attacked the group, cutting off their hands, ears, and noses. Then he sent them back to Orchomenus.

Trouble followed Hercules. King Erginus (er-JIH-nuhs) of the Minyans sent his army. They waited at the gates of Thebes and demanded that Creon (KREE-on), the Theban king, send Hercules out.

Chapter 2

Hercules wanted to fight. He convinced some other young men to join him. The Minyans had taken all of the Thebans' weapons to stop them from fighting back. But Hercules knew where several weapons remained. He and the other Thebans raided a temple where old weapons and armor had been left years before as an offering to the gods. The men dusted off the swords, spears, and shields.

When Hercules heard that King Erginus and his army were heading towards Thebes, "he went out to meet him in a certain narrow place," wrote the historian Diodorus Siculus (dahy-oh-DAWR-uhs SIK-yuh-luhs). Hercules "killed Erginus himself, and slew [killed] practically all the men who had accompanied him. Then . . . he burned the palace of the Minyans and **razed** the city to the ground."[2]

King Creon was very grateful. He let Hercules marry his oldest daughter, Megara (MEG-er-uh). Her sister married Hercules's brother.

Hercules's Happy Home
Hercules settled down. He had a nice home, a wife, and very soon, three sons. Life was perfect. Unfortunately, he still had a powerful enemy.

Juno had never forgiven Jupiter. One day, she decided to make Hercules crazy—so crazy that he believed his wife and sons were enemy soldiers. He fought them. He fought everyone. He killed and killed.

The goddess Minerva (mi-NUR-vuh), ruler of wisdom, finally stepped in. She hit Hercules with a boulder and knocked him out. When he woke up, he saw for the first time what he had really done. He had killed his wife. He had killed his three young boys.

A Hero Is Born

Hercules's sudden madness led him to kill his wife Megara (left) and their children. This 1,800-year-old mosaic panel showing the event is displayed at the National Archaeology Museum in Lisbon, Portugal.

Chapter 2

Now Hercules had a new reason to go crazy. He cried and he wanted to die. He begged for punishment, but no punishment came.

Finally, Hercules left. He visited the one person who could tell him what to do. She was the oracle of Delphi. Oracles told people what was going to happen. They also gave advice. Outside the Temple of Apollo, Hercules made a **sacrifice**. Then he entered.

The oracle breathed in the strange gas flooding the temple. She saw what Hercules must do.

To be forgiven, he must give up his freedom. The strongest man on the planet must become a slave. Worst of all, he would be told what to do by the king of Mycenae. Eurystheus had become king instead of Hercules only because Juno had made sure he was born first. Soon he would also be Hercules's master.

Called the Pythia, the oracle of the Temple of Apollo at Delphi was regularly asked for her advice in Ancient Greece. Here, she is shown seated on a three-legged stool as she breathes in the gases rising from the ground.

History or Just a Story?

Most historians today agree that the gods and goddesses like Jupiter and Juno didn't exist. But some people think that Hercules might have actually lived in ancient Greece.

Many of the ancient Greek historians discuss Hercules as if he was a real man. In the fifth century BCE, Herodotus (huh-ROD-uh-tuhs) traveled to Scythia (SITH-ee-uh), a region in eastern Europe and western Asia. The locals showed him a rock which had the mark of a very large human footprint. They reported that the footprint was made by Hercules himself. Herodotus says that this mark is one of the only things in the land that is "worthy of note."[3]

Historians estimate that if Hercules was real, he would have been born around the thirteenth century BCE. The stories of real events might have been exaggerated as they were told over hundreds of years. However, Hercules's many adventures take place at different times in history. Some people think that this is because there were actually two or three people named Hercules who lived at different times. The stories of these men might have been combined into a single story.

Today, we can't prove whether Hercules did or didn't exist. Ancient writings can only tell us what people believed thousands of years ago. Despite this, many people think it's possible that the stories of Hercules began with a real man.

Herodotus

Hercules's first job for King Eurystheus was to kill the Nemean lion. It turned out to be more difficult than Hercules had thought.

3
LABORS OF A HERO

The king was unhappy. Having the strongest man on the planet to do everything he asked sounded awesome. Except King Eurystheus knew what Hercules had done. He worried that a man who could kill his own family would have no problem killing a king.

The king decided that Hercules would have to do ten labors, or jobs, before he could be free again. The first job he gave Hercules was a dangerous one. He didn't just want Hercules to fail. He wanted him to die. King Eurystheus sent Hercules to kill the man-eating Nemean (NEE-mee-uhn) lion.

Hercules was not worried. He'd already killed one deadly lion. Another should be no problem. This one was easier to find, at least. When he had tracked the lion down, Hercules crept up and aimed his bow. The arrow's aim was true.

It bounced off the lion! Hercules fired again. The same thing happened. The lion didn't even seem to notice. Like Hercules, the lion was related to the gods.

Hercules had to try something different. He picked up his club and attacked.

Chapter 3

The lion fled into a cave. Since the cave had two entrances, Hercules couldn't just follow the lion. He needed to trap it inside the cave. So he pushed rocks in front of one entrance, and went into the cave through the other. When the lion was finally cornered, Hercules grabbed it around the neck and squeezed. He was stronger than the lion. Hercules choked it to death. Then he used the lion's own claws to slice off its hide. Now he had armor. The animal's skin would protect Hercules from weapons.

He wore the hide back to Mycenae, but the king was not impressed. He was terrified. "Amazed at his manhood," Apollodorus wrote, "Eurystheus forbade him thenceforth to enter the city, but ordered him to exhibit [show] the fruits of his labors before the gates."[1] From now on, a messenger would give Hercules his orders.

A Monster, a Deer, and a Boar

The hero's next job was more dangerous than the first. A monster lived near a town called Lerna (LUR-nuh), and Hercules would have to kill it. Called the Hydra (HAHY-druh), it looked like an eel or a snake. Except a snake has one head. The Hydra had nine!

Hercules traveled to Lerna in a chariot with his nephew Iolaus (ay-oh-LAY-uhs). There, he found the Hydra in its den on a hillside. He shot flaming arrows into the den to force the Hydra to come out.

Drawing his sword, he ran to the monster. In a flash of metal against skin, Hercules sliced off a head. The head fell to the ground. Hercules watched as two more heads grew in its place. He cut another head off. More heads grew. Now the monster had eleven heads, and it was growing

LABORS OF A HERO

stronger and angrier. Worse, a giant crab came to help the Hydra by pinching Hercules's foot. It was obvious that this plan was not going to work.

Hercules needed to use his own head. He went back to the chariot to come up with a plan. Iolaus was waiting for him there. Hercules told Iolaus to build a fire. When the fire was burning, Hercules stuck his club into the flames and the club became a torch. He handed it to his nephew.

In 1876, Gustave Moreau painted this image of Hercules confronting the Hydra.

Chapter 3

The two approached the Hydra. As the beast attacked, Hercules swung his sword. When the animal lost a head, Iolaus held the torch to the stump. This burned the neck so a new head could not grow.

In minutes, Hercules had killed a creature many believed would never die. His reward? Nothing. When he returned to Mycenae, the king said this labor did not count. Hercules had received help.

His third job was not dangerous. He had to catch a deer, but he did not want to kill or hurt it. The deer had horns made of gold and was very special to the goddess Diana. For a year, Hercules chased the deer. When he finally caught up with the animal, it looked as though it would escape again by crossing a stream. Hercules wasn't about to let that happen. He shot the deer.

The deer was still alive, but it couldn't run from Hercules any longer. He picked it up and was heading back to Mycenae when Diana confronted him. She was very angry that Hercules had almost killed her deer. Apologizing, Hercules explained that he was ordered to bring the deer back to Eurystheus. It took some convincing, but the goddess eventually allowed Hercules to borrow her pet.

Upon Hercules's return, King Eurystheus released the golden deer so it could go home to Diana. Then he sent Hercules after another animal. This one was not as gentle.

In the shadows of Mount Erymanthus (er-uh-MAN-thuhs), a boar was killing the townspeople. Reaching the boar took Hercules on a long journey across steep mountain paths. It was hard work, even for someone whose dad was Jupiter. He needed a break. A friendly centaur named Pholus (FOH-luhs) invited Hercules into his cave. He offered him a cooked meal and a place to sleep.

LABORS OF A HERO

Hercules enjoyed the food. He asked for some wine, but Pholus said he couldn't offer it. The wine belonged to all the centaurs. Hercules insisted.

Reluctantly, Pholus opened the wine. Apollodorus wrote, "not long afterwards, scenting the smell, the centaurs arrived at the cave of Pholus, armed with rocks and firs."[2] Hercules was drunk and angry. He began fighting the beasts. He killed most of them, including his host. Worse, his childhood teacher Chiron was injured. Hercules had used arrows dipped in the Hydra's poison. Because Chiron was immortal, his pain was unending. Eventually he traded with the god Prometheus (pruh-MEE-thee-uhs), who took Chiron's immortality so the centaur could die in peace.

After his teacher's death, Hercules went after the boar. He chased the beast right into a snowbank. It was quick work for him to tie it up and take it back to the king. When the ruler saw Hercules carrying the boar, he hid inside a huge bronze jar, buried in the ground.

King Eurystheus was so frightened by the sight of Hercules and the boar, that he hid in a giant jar.

CHAPTER 3

Hercules Cleans Up!

Hercules's fifth job would take him to King Augeas (aw-JEE-uhs) of Elis. The king had more sheep and cattle than any other man on earth. Yet even the poorest rancher took better care of his animals. King Augeas kept his herds in huge stables. The stables had not been cleaned in years. Cleaning the stables was a dirty job and Hercules had to do it in just one day.

When Hercules arrived, King Augeas did not know that Eurystheus had sent him to clean the stables. Hercules told the king that he would clean the stables in just one day, but he wanted some of the king's herd in exchange. The king laughed—it was impossible. But he agreed. If Hercules succeeded, he could have some of the herd.

The royal stables were filthy and neglected. Hercules tore down one wall. Then he tore down the wall it faced. He walked to the nearby River Alpheus (al-FEE-uhs). Hercules pulled down tree branches and piled up dirt in the middle of the river. The water overflowed the banks. It raced toward the stables and soon it had washed away the filth.

The stables were spotless. Hercules took down his dam and went back to King Augeas. The king refused to pay. Hercules was angry, but he returned to Mycenae to wait for another task.

King Eurystheus was unimpressed. Hercules had asked for payment so the king said the labor did not count. Hercules still had seven labors left. He could not imagine them getting worse. But they would.

The Olympics

More than any other event, the Olympic Games connect the modern world with ancient Greece. Today the winter and summer competitions happen every four years. Representing their countries, the best athletes from around the world compete for medals. Events include ice skating, boxing, gymnastics, and track and field.

According to written records, the Olympics began in Greece in 776 BCE. Athletes from different city-states competed in the event, which started out as a foot race. More competitions were added over time, and eventually the Olympics lasted five days. All free male Greek citizens could participate. Although women did not compete, unmarried women could watch the event alongside Greek men. Some of the earliest competitions were running, wrestling, and chariot racing.

In mythology, Hercules never forgot that King Augeas had refused to pay him for cleaning the stables. After he had finished all his labors, Hercules returned to kill the king in revenge. He started the athletic competition to celebrate his victory. Hercules even planted an olive tree so that its branches could be used to make crowns for the winners. "And he stipulated [required] that the prize in them should be only a crown, since he himself had conferred benefits upon the race of men [helped people] without receiving any monetary reward [money]," wrote historian Diodorus Siculus.[3]

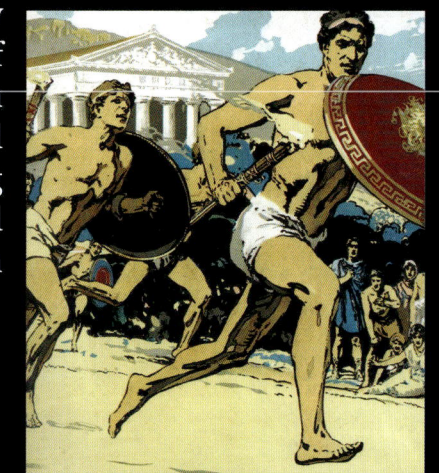

Ancient Olympic Games, the relay race

Hercules has appeared on ancient coins and modern stamps. Here he is shown confronting the Stamphalian birds on a Greek stamp issued in 1970.

4

Final Labors

Being a hero can be for the birds. Hercules learned this in Arcadia (ahr-KEY-dee-uh), where a flock of deadly birds lived along Lake Stymphalia (stim-FEY-lee-uh). There were thousands of them, with feathers as sharp as Hercules's sword. Their beaks and claws could cut through metal. No one was safe.

Hercules knew he could not fight them as he had the Hydra or the Minyans. "It was not possible to master the animals by force because of the exceptional multitude [great number] of them," wrote the historian Diodorus Siculus, "and so the deed called for [cleverness]. . . ."[1] Hercules made a large rattle out of bronze and shook it. The sound scared the birds so badly, they left and never returned.

His next task was capturing a bull in Crete (KREET). Created by Neptune, the sea god, the bull was a gift to King Minos (MAHY-nuhs). When the king did not sacrifice it, Neptune was very angry. He made the bull go wild. It was attacking people all over the island. King Eurystheus wanted Hercules to bring it back. This was hardly a challenge for Hercules. He soon brought the bull back to Mycenae.

Chapter 4

This time, King Eurystheus sent Hercules further away. He would go to Thrace (THREYS) and bring back King Diomedes's (dahy-uh-MEE-deez) horses.

On the way, Hercules was invited to stay at the home of Admetus (ad-MEE-tuhs), a king in Thessaly. He soon noticed that everyone was sad because the queen had just died. So Hercules visited the queen's grave. It was guarded by Thanatos (THAN-uh-tos), who was death itself. Hercules wrestled Thanatos to the ground and the queen came back to life.

After winning a fight with death, catching a few horses should have been easy. Except these were not just any horses. King Diomedes did not feed them grain or hay. He fed them human flesh. The horses were mean and dangerous, but Hercules was unafraid.

He realized what the horses really wanted and he gave them a meal they had never had before. He fed them King Diomedes. After that, the horses followed Hercules back to Mycenae.

Amazons and Gods

King Eurystheus was frustrated. Hercules was facing his ninth labor. So far nothing had bothered him. The king had run out of ideas.

The king's daughter, Admete (ad-MEE-tee), knew what she wanted. She asked Hercules to bring her a special belt made of gold. It was worn by Hippolyta (hi-PAHL-i-tuh), the queen of the Amazons. Amazons were very powerful women who did not allow men to live with them. When a boy was born to an Amazon, he was given away or left outdoors to die.

Final Labors

Hercules knew the Amazons were great warriors. So when he went to their queen, he did not attack her. Instead, he invited her onto his ship and told her his story. When he finished his tale, Queen Hippolyta handed over her belt.

The task seemed like it had been easy. Except Hercules had forgotten about the most dangerous woman in his life. While he had been talking with Hippolyta, Juno had disguised herself as an Amazon. She told the others that Hercules and his men were trying to kidnap their queen. The Amazons got on their horses and charged, believing they were rescuing Hippolyta. Hercules saw the attacking Amazons, and he thought the queen had tricked him. He killed her and sailed off with the belt.

Admete loved the belt. And her father had come up with another task for Hercules. The next job took Hercules to Spain where he captured the cows from the three-bodied giant. On his way home, he would slay Cacus.

By now, Hercules had completed ten labors. But two of them didn't count. So he would have to continue on. Job number eleven was to bring King Eurystheus three golden apples. Not the kind that you'd buy in a store. These apples were made of real gold. The tree they grew on was guarded by a dragon. Worse, the tree belonged to Juno!

The first problem Hercules had was that he didn't know where to find the garden. He set out to find someone who could tell him where the apples were. After traveling through North Africa and the Middle East, he found Prometheus. The god had tried to help humans, against Jupiter's wishes. So Jupiter had left him chained to

Chapter 4

a mountain. Every day, an eagle came to eat Prometheus's liver. His liver grew back again before the eagle returned the next day.

Hercules killed the eagle and released Prometheus from his chains. The god was grateful. Even better, he knew exactly how Hercules could get the apples. Prometheus explained that the guardians of the garden were the Hesperides (he-SPER-i-deez). Prometheus's brother Atlas was their father. Atlas would have no problem getting the apples with help from his daughters.

So Hercules visited Atlas. He had the weight of the world on his shoulders—literally! Greeks and Romans believed the earth and the sky were held up by Atlas. Hercules offered the god a break. He would take on the weight of the world while Atlas took on the dragon guarding the apple tree. The god agreed.

When Atlas returned with the apples, he had bad news. He did not like holding up the world. He would take the apples to Mycenae. But he was leaving Hercules stuck with the world on his back.

Now Hercules was not the brightest of Jupiter's children. Still, this time he outsmarted a god. He

The tortured god Prometheus, as seen in this statue in Vienna, Austria.

Final Labors

asked if Atlas would hold the world just long enough to let him get a cushion to put between the earth and his shoulders. Since he would be there a long time, he wanted to be comfortable. Atlas agreed. He put down the apples and picked up the world. But as soon as he did, Hercules picked up the apples and left Atlas holding up the world!

Labors' End

Back in Mycenae, the king said there were no more jobs for Hercules left in the world. His last job would be in the underworld. Romans believed when people died, they went to the underworld, which was ruled by Pluto. The living did not visit this dark and scary place. But Hercules would need to go there and return with the three-headed, dragon-tailed dog named Cerberus (SUR-ber-uhs). This animal guarded the gates of the underworld to make sure that no spirits escaped.

Hercules made his way to the cave that led to the underworld. Because he had killed many people, Hercules knew there was a chance he would not return. When he reached Pluto's throne, he was humble. He did not want to be stuck there. He only had one request: to borrow the dog.

Atlas holding up the world

Chapter 4

Pluto allowed Hercules to take the dog on one condition. He could not use any weapons, only his bare hands. The fight was epic. In the end, Hercules was stronger than Cerberus. He brought the dog back to King Eurystheus, then returned it to its home. The jobs were done. Hercules was free!

For his last labor, Hercules had to fight the three-headed dog Cerberus that guarded the gates of the underworld. The fight is shown in this etching from 1606.

Constellations

In the stories of Hercules, many constellations were created. Constellations are groups of stars that form patterns in the sky. After Hercules killed the Nemean lion, Juno sent it into the sky to become the constellation Leo. The giant crab also became a constellation. Hercules killed it, then flung it into the sky where it formed the constellation Cancer. After his death, Hercules himself became a constellation.

People around the world looked up at the sky and saw different patterns. Many of them used these patterns and their position in the sky to know exactly what time of year it was. This was especially useful for farmers, who planted crops in the spring. Paintings on cave walls show that people may have been studying clusters of stars over seventeen thousand years ago.[2]

In the second century CE, the Greek **astronomer** Ptolemy (TOL-uh-mee) wrote the *Almagest* (AL-muh-jest), which listed many of the constellations we know today. However people around the world were using their own groups of stars, all with different names. As scientists began to work together to study the stars, they realized that an official set of constellations was needed. In 1922, the International Astronomical Union named eighty-eight constellations that everyone in the world could use.

Hercules constellation

Hercules was a skilled hunter and warrior who used the most advanced weapons of his time, including the bow and arrow. Here his talent is shown in a gilded bronze statue displayed in Paris, France.

5
Death of a Hero

Hercules was no longer a slave. Now he wanted a family. King Eurytus, who had taught Hercules to use a bow and arrow, was holding an archery contest. The king would let the best archer marry his daughter, Iole (AY-uh-lee). The contest was perfect!

Hercules won easily, but it didn't matter. The king knew his **reputation**. He was not going to take a chance on Iole being killed the way Megara had been. He refused to reward Hercules.

Hercules was angry. Soon, the king's horses disappeared and everyone suspected Hercules was to blame. The king's son went to Hercules's home to look for the missing animals. Hercules welcomed the prince and showed him around. High walls offered the best view. Hercules told the prince to climb atop them. While the king's son looked around, Hercules pushed him off.

Hercules had killed the king's son. He had also stolen the king's horses.

Soon, Hercules began to get very sick. Hoping to be cured, he visited the oracle at Delphi. The oracle refused to help him. She didn't think he'd learned anything from

CHAPTER 5

being a slave. Enraged, Hercules attacked the oracle. He wrecked the temple. When the god Apollo tried to stop him, the two fought.

The oracle finally told Hercules that he was sick because he had murdered the king's son. The only way to cure the disease was to become a slave again. This time, he served Queen Omphale (AHM-fuh-lee). They got along very well together. During his time with her, Hercules had many more adventures.

After three years, Hercules was again a free man. He still wanted a family. He fell in love with a woman named Deianira (dee-yuh-NAHY-ruh). But nothing seemed to come to Hercules without a fight. A river god also wanted to marry her. The god turned himself into a bull and attacked Hercules. After Hercules broke the bull's horn, he married Deianira.

Hercules's second marriage to Deianira would be as unhappy as his first. The wedding is shown here on a sixteenth-century plate.

Death of a Hero

A Centaur's Betrayal

A few years later, the couple was traveling together and came to a river. A centaur named Nessus (NES-uhs) was selling ferry rides across the river. Hercules paid for his wife to cross, but he decided to swim. As they crossed the river, Nessus tried to hurt Deianira and she screamed for Hercules. The hero shot Nessus in the heart.

As he lay dying, Nessus told Deianira to collect his blood and save it. She could use it in case her husband ever loved another woman. The blood would make Hercules love his wife again.

Hercules Beating the Centaur Nessus *by Giambologna*

Chapter 5

Meanwhile, Hercules hadn't forgotten about King Eurytus. He was still angry that the king hadn't honored his promise. Hercules also thought it was Eurytus's fault that he had to become a slave again. He was ready to get revenge.

Hercules led a group of men to attack King Eurytus. After he killed the king, he took Iole. Hercules then sent his messenger home for a special shirt. When the messenger arrived, he told Deianira all that had happened. She was not happy. She was afraid her husband no longer loved her. Before she sent Hercules the shirt he wanted, she soaked it in Nessus's blood.

The centaur had lied. When Hercules wore the shirt, he was poisoned. His death was slow and painful. He begged one of his men to kill him, but no one would. So Hercules stacked up piles of wood. He climbed on top and told the men to set the wood on fire. As Hercules began to die a mortal death, Jupiter saved his son. A chariot carried him to his new home among the stars.

Hercules Goes to Rome

In Rome, Hercules's life was celebrated. Every year on August 12, Rome held a festival for Hercules. The city sacrificed oxen to the man who once stole cattle for a king.

Romans used festivals to honor gods, goddesses, and heroes. There were many festivals during the year. Few people worked or went to school on festival days, so not much got done. Still, most people in Rome believed it was important to honor the gods so good things would happen.

By the first century BCE, the Roman Empire had become quite large. It ruled people in many places, and many of them prayed to their own gods. The Romans encouraged

Hercules' rescue from mortal death is shown in this painting, *The Apotheosis of Hercules*, which is located at the famous French Palace of Versailles.

Chapter 5

people to continue worshiping their local gods, and also introduced their own. But soon, a new religion called Christianity was spreading throughout the empire.

When there were problems in the empire, Christians were often blamed. The Roman leaders believed that if people ignored the Roman gods, the gods would stop protecting the empire. Christians were ordered to light **incense** in front of the emperor's statue as a form of prayer. Many Christians refused. They were often tortured and killed.

In 313 CE, the emperor Constantine granted Romans the freedom to practice Christianity. Theodosius made Christianity the Roman Empire's official state religion in 380 CE.

By then, Hercules was remembered for his bravery and his constellations. People weren't praying to him any longer. Yet stories about his amazing adventures have endured for thousands of years.

Although half human, Hercules was honored like a god at the Temple of Hercules in Rome, Italy.

Hercules in the 21st Century

Thousands of years ago, people were entertained by storytellers. Today, people go into a darkened theater and watch huge monsters and terrifying demons. Since movies began, not many myths from Ancient Greece and Rome have been as popular as Hercules. With his large muscles, Hercules is the perfect movie hero.

His size is one reason many famous bodybuilders have played Hercules. Lou Ferrigno became well known as the Hulk. A few years later, he played Hercules. So too did Arnold Schwarzenegger, over ten years before he became famous as the Terminator. In 2014, former pro wrestler Dwayne Johnson tackled the role of Hercules.

Although other actors have played Hercules, many people picture Steve Reeves when they think of the hero. At six-foot-one and 215 pounds, he was ideal for the part. The Mr. Universe winner had little luck finding acting work in Hollywood. Instead, his big break came in Italy when he was cast as Hercules in a 1958 film. He went on to star as the hero of many more films over the next decade. At one point, he was the highest paid actor in Europe.

There have been many versions of Hercules's story. Still, many people consider the best version to be a cartoon, Walt Disney's 1997 film, *Hercules*.

Steve Reeves in the 1959 movie Hercules Unchained

Chapter Notes

Chapter 1: Epic Battle
1. Virgil, *Aeneid*, Book 8, trans. C. Day Lewis, in Theoi Project, "Kakos," http://www.theoi.com/Gigante/GiganteKakos.html

Chapter 2: A Hero is Born
1. Apollodorus, *The Library*, Book 2, trans. J.G. Frazer, in Theoi Project, "Apollodorus, Library 2," http://www.theoi.com/Text/Apollodorus2.html
2. Diodorus Siculus, *Library of History*, Book 4, trans. C.H. Oldfather (Cambridge, MA: Harvard University Press, 1935), 10.5, in Theoi Project, "Diodorus Siculus IV. 1–18," http://www.theoi.com/Text/DiodorusSiculus4A.html
3. Herodotus, *The History of Herodotus*, Book 4, trans. George Rawlinson, Internet Classics Archive, http://classics.mit.edu/Herodotus/history.4.iv.html

Chapter 3: Labors of a Hero
1. Apollodorus, *The Library*, Book 2, trans. J.G. Frazer, in Theoi Project, "Apollodorus, Library 2," http://www.theoi.com/Text/Apollodorus2.html
2. Ibid.
3. Diodorus Siculus, *Library of History*, Book 4, trans. C.H. Oldfather (Cambridge, MA: Harvard University Press, 1935), 14.1, in Theoi Project, "Diodorus Siculus IV. 1–18," http://www.theoi.com/Text/DiodorusSiculus4A.html

Chapter 4: Final Labors
1. Diodorus Siculus, *Library of History*, Book 4, trans. C.H. Oldfather (Cambridge, MA: Harvard University Press, 1935), 13.2, in Theoi Project, "Diodorus Siculus IV. 1–18," http://www.theoi.com/Text/DiodorusSiculus4A.html
2. International Astronomical Union, "The Constellations," http://www.iau.org/public/themes/constellations/

Works Consulted

Apollodorus. *The Library*. Book 2. Translated by J.G. Frazer. In Theoi Project. "Apollodorus, Library 2." http://www.theoi.com/Text/Apollodorus2.html

Bulfinch, Thomas. *Bulfinch's Mythology*. New York: The Modern Library, 2004.

Day, Malcolm. *100 Characters from Classical Mythology: Discover the Fascinating Stories of the Greek and Roman Deities*. London: Quarto, 2007.

Diodorus Siculus. *Library of History*. Book 4. Translated by C.H. Oldfather. Cambridge, MA: Harvard University Press, 1935. In Theoi Project. "Diodorus Siculus IV. 1-18." http://www.theoi.com/Text/DiodorusSiculus4A.html

Works Consulted

Finn, Thomas M. *From Death to Rebirth: Ritual and Conversion in Antiquity.* Mahwah, NJ: Paulist Press, 1997.
Forty, Jo. *Classic Mythology.* London: Grange, 1999.
Freeman, Philip. *Oh My Gods: A Modern Retelling of Greek and Roman Myths.* New York: Simon & Schuster, 2012.
Hamilton, Edith. *Mythology.* New York: Spark Pub., 2007.
Herodotus. *The History of Herodotus.* Book 4. Translated by George Rawlinson. Internet Classics Archive. http://classics.mit.edu/Herodotus/history.4.iv.html
International Astronomical Union. "The Constellations." http://www.iau.org/public/themes/constellations/
National Geographic. *The Lost Gospel of Judas.* "Roman Emperors Persecute Christians: A.D. 30 to 313." http://www.nationalgeographic.com/lostgospel/timeline_09.html
Olympic.org. "Ancient Olympic Games." http://www.olympic.org/ancient-olympic-games
PBS. *The Roman Empire in the First Century.* "Early Christians." http://www.pbs.org/empires/romans/empire/christians.html
Virgil. *Aeneid.* Book 8. Translated by C. Day Lewis. In Theoi Project. "Kakos." http://www.theoi.com/Gigante/GiganteKakos.html

Further Reading

Allan, Tony. *Exploring the Life, Myth, and Art of Ancient Rome.* New York: Rosen Pub., 2012.
Jennings, Ken. *Greek Mythology.* New York: Little Simon, 2014.
McCaughrean, Geraldine. *Hercules.* Chicago: Cricket Books, 2005.
Van Lente, Fred. *Hercules.* Oxford, UK: Osprey Publishing, 2013.

On the Internet

International Astronomical Union: The Constellations
    http://www.iau.org/public/themes/constellations/
Kidipede: Herakles
    http://www.historyforkids.org/learn/greeks/religion/myths/herakles.htm
NASA: Make a Star Finder (Constellations)
    http://spaceplace.nasa.gov/starfinder/en/
Olympic.org: Ancient Olympic Games
    http://www.olympic.org/ancient-olympic-games?tab=history

PHOTO CREDITS: All design elements from Thinkstock/Sharon Beck. Cover, pp. 1, 4, 27, 28, 35—Thinkstock; p. 7—Jonthan Scott/Tammy West; pp. 9, 10, 13, 14, 17, 19, 20, 23, 25, 32, 33, 34, 36, 38, 39, 41—cc-by-sa; p. 18—World History Archive/Newscom; p. 42—Frank Bach/Dreamstime; p. 43—LUX/GALATEA/Album/Newscom.

Glossary

aqueduct (AK-wi-duhkt)—a structure built to carry water over long distances, using gravity

archery (AHR-chuh-ree)—the practice of shooting with a bow and arrow

astronomer (uh-STRON-uh-mer)—a scientist who studies the universe outside of the earth, including stars, moons, and planets

city-state—a city in ancient Greece that was ruled independently

epic poem—a very long poem that usually tells the story of a hero

incense (IN-sens)—a gum or other substance that smells sweet when it is burned, sometimes used in a religious ritual like an offering to a god

javelin (JAV-uh-lin)—a very light spear that is thrown as a weapon or in a sporting event

ogre (OH-ger)—a large, ugly monster that eats humans

raze (REYZ)—to tear down or destroy

reputation (rep-yuh-TEY-shuhn)—what other people think about a person, often based on the person's past actions

sacrifice (SAK-ruh-fahys)—something of value (like an animal or plant) that is given to honor or please a god or goddess, or to get something else from the god or goddess in return

Index

Admete 30, 31
Admetus (king) 30
Alcmene 11–12
Almagest 35
Alpheus (river) 26
Amazons 7, 30–31
Amphitryon 11–12, 14
Apollo 38
Apollodorus 15, 22, 25
Apollo, Temple of 18, 38
aqueducts 9
Arcadia 29
archery 12, 21, 22, 24, 25, 36, 37, 39
architecture 9
Athens 7, 8
Atlas 32–33
Augeias (king) 26, 27
Bible 23
birds 28, 29
boar 25
bull 29, 38
Cacus 4, 5–6, 8, 31
cattle 5–6, 11, 14, 15, 26, 31, 40
centaurs 13, 14, 24–25, 39, 40
Cerberus 33–34
chariots 12, 22, 23, 27, 40
Chiron 13, 14, 25
Christianity 42
Cithaeron, Mount 7, 15
city-states 8, 11, 27
Constantine 42
constellations 35, 42
crab 23, 35
Creon (king) 15, 16

INDEX

Crete 7, 29
deer 24
Deianira 38–40
Delphi 7, 18, 37–38
Diana 24
Diomedes (king) 30
dogs 5, 33–34
eagle 32
Egypt 7, 8
Electryon (king) 11
Elis 7, 26
England 8
Erginus (king) 15, 16
Erymanthus, Mount 7, 24
Eurystheus (king) 12, 18, 20, 21, 22, 24, 25, 26, 29–30, 31, 33, 34
Eurytus (king) 12, 37, 40
Ferrigno, Lou 43
fire 23–24
Geryon 5, 31
golden apples 31–33
Greece and Greeks 6, 7, 8, 10, 11, 12, 13, 15, 18, 19, 27, 28, 32, 35, 43
Hercules (Heracles)
    birth 12
    childhood 12–14
    children 16
    constellation 35
    death 40, 41
    labors 5–6, 18, 20, 21–26, 27, 28, 29–34, 35
    marriages 16, 17, 38–40
    slavery 18, 20, 21–26, 27, 28, 29–34, 35, 38, 40
    temple 42

Herodotus 19
Hesperides 7, 32
Hippolyta (queen) 30–31
Homer 7
horses 12, 30, 37
Hydra 22–24, 25, 29
Iliad 7
International Astronomical Union 35
Iolaus 22–24
Iole 37, 40
Iphicles 12
Johnson, Dwayne 43
Juno (Hera) 7, 12, 16, 18, 19, 31, 35
Jupiter (Zeus) 7, 12, 15, 16, 19, 24, 31, 32, 40
kraters 10, 14
Leo 35
Lerna 7, 22–24
Linus 13–14
lions 15, 20, 21–22
lyre 13
Macedonia 7
Mediterranean Sea 8
Megara 16, 17, 37
Minerva 16
Minos (king) 29
Minyans 15–16, 29
movies 43
Mycenae 7, 11, 12, 18, 22, 24, 26, 29, 30, 32, 33
mythology 6–7, 19
Nemean lion 7, 20, 21–22, 35
Neptune 29
Nessus 39, 40
Odyssey 7
ogre 4, 5–6
olive tree 27
Olympians 7

Olympic Games 27
Olympus, Mount 7
Omphale (queen) 38
oracle of Delphi 18, 37–38
Orchomenus 7, 15
Palatine Hill 8
Perseus 12
Pholus 24–25
Plato 6
Pluto 33–34
Prometheus 25, 31–32
Ptolemy 35
Pythia 18
Reeves, Steve 43
Roman Empire 8, 40, 41
Rome and Romans 5, 6, 7, 8, 9, 12, 32, 33, 40, 42, 43
Schwarzenegger, Arnold 43
Scythia 19
sheep 26
Siculus, Diodorus 16, 27, 29
snakes 12, 13
Spain 5, 7, 8, 31
Sparta 7, 8
stables 26, 27
Sthenelus 11
Stymphalia, Lake 28
Taphos 7, 11
Thanatos 30
Thebes 7, 11, 15–16
Theodosius 42
Thespius (king) 15
Thessaly 7, 30
Thrace 7, 30
Titans 7
Turkey 7, 8
underworld 33–34
Virgil 5–6
wine 25

About the Author

Born in Boston, Massachusetts, John Bankston began writing articles while still a teenager. Since then, over two hundred of his articles have been published in magazines and newspapers across the country, including travel articles in *The Tallahassee Democrat*, *The Orlando Sentinel*, and *The Tallahassean*. He is the author of over sixty biographies for young adults, including Alexander the Great, scientist Stephen Hawking, author F. Scott Fitzgerald, and actor Jodie Foster.